I0816754
NATIONAL PARKS
GLACIER
Heather Kissock
AV2
www.av2books.com

Step 1
Go to **www.av2books.com**

Step 2
Enter this unique code
KXPEYG9HU

Step 3
Explore your interactive eBook!

AV2 is optimized for use on any device

Your interactive eBook comes with...

Contents
Browse a live contents page to easily navigate through resources

Audio
Listen to sections of the book read aloud

Videos
Watch informative video clips

Weblinks
Gain additional information for research

Slideshows
View images and captions

Try This!
Complete activities and hands-on experiments

Key Words
Study vocabulary, and complete a matching word activity

Quizzes
Test your knowledge

Share
Share titles within your Learning Management System (LMS) or Library Circulation System

Citation
Create bibliographical references following the Chicago Manual of Style

This title is part of our AV2 digital subscription

1-Year 3–8 Subscription
ISBN 978-1-7911-3306-1

Access hundreds of AV2 titles with our digital subscription.
Sign up for a FREE trial at **www.av2books.com/trial**

CONTENTS

Crown of the Continent

Vibrant scenery is a hallmark of Glacier National Park. Tall mountains rise majestically toward the sky, their peaks often capped with snow. Pristine lakes shimmer a crystal blue. Wildlife roam the dense forests and open clearings. It is no wonder that about 3 million people come to visit this park every year.

Located in northern Montana, Glacier National Park covers an area of 1,583 square miles (4,100 square kilometers). The park was named for its many **glaciers**. However, the number of glaciers has decreased due to **climate change**. In 1850, the park had about 150 glaciers. Today, only 26 remain.

Grinnell Lake is one of the many glacier-fed lakes in Glacier National Park.

Harrison Glacier is the largest glacier in the park. It spans an area of 17.9 million square feet (1.7 million square meters). Other glaciers of note include the Blackfoot and Jackson Glaciers. The park's glaciers are popular with visitors. Some take a sightseeing drive through the park to view them from afar. Others hike into the backcountry for an up-close experience.

The Harrison and Jackson glaciers both sit on Mount Jackson. At 10,052 feet (3,064 m), this mountain is the fourth tallest in the park.

MAPPING GLACIER

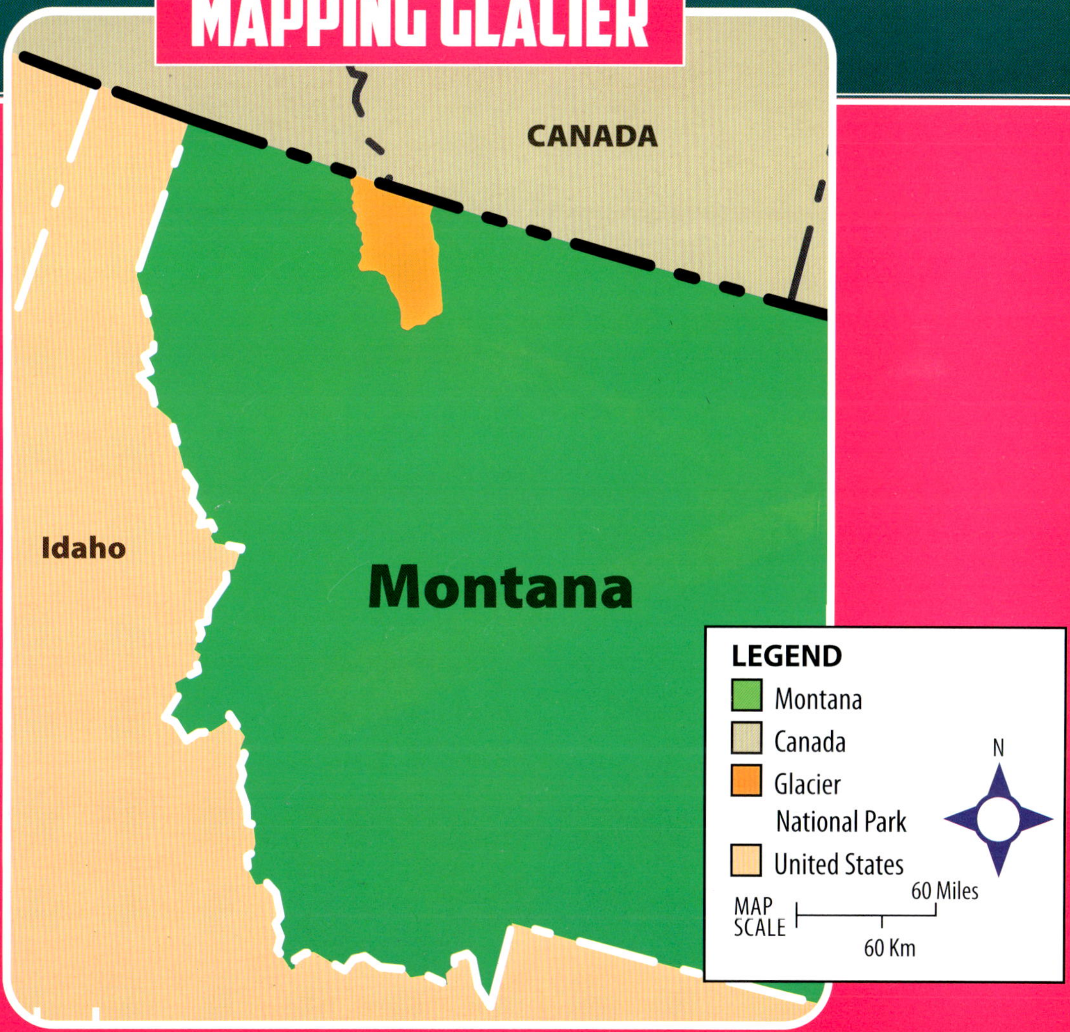

CANADA

Idaho

Montana

LEGEND

- Montana
- Canada
- Glacier National Park
- United States

N

MAP SCALE 60 Miles 60 Km

Where Is Glacier?

Glacier National Park sits along the United States–Canada border. Across the border from it is Canada's Waterton Lakes National Park. Together, Glacier and Waterton form the Waterton-Glacier International Peace Park. Founded in 1932, it is the world's first International Peace Park. Along with showcasing the peaceful relationship between the two countries, the park demonstrates how nations can work together to preserve their natural wonders.

The Rocky Mountains, or Rockies, run through both parks. This mountain chain extends from Canada all the way south to New Mexico, covering a distance of about 3,000 miles (4,800 km). The Continental Divide also runs through Glacier National Park. The divide separates the Atlantic and Pacific **watersheds**. Waters on the west side of the divide drain into the Pacific Ocean. Waters on the east side flow toward the Atlantic Ocean.

The Canadian town of Waterton sits along the shores of Waterton Lake. The lake straddles the border between Waterton Lakes National Park and Glacier National Park.

PUZZLER

The Rockies run through at least seven American states, two Canadian provinces, and two Canadian territories.

Q: Can you identify each of the locations on the map below?

A Rocky Start

Mountains are formed when the **tectonic plates** that make up Earth's crust move. The Rockies began to form between 80 and 55 million years ago. This was when two plates, the Pacific and the North American, began to push against each other. Part of the Pacific plate went underneath the more buoyant North American plate. The collision pushed huge slabs of rock upward and over each other. It was this action that created the Rocky Mountains.

The mountains continued to change shape over time. Much of this change was due to erosion from glacier movement. During the last **ice age**, which took place between 2.6 million and 11,700 years ago, a series of glaciers moved over the continent. They carved into the mountain rock, forming the valleys, moraines, and passes found in the Rockies today.

Wynn Mountain is one of the best places to see evidence of the mountain-building activity that took place millions of years ago. The base of the mountain shows clear signs of older rock folded over newer rock.

MOUNTAIN TYPES

Earth's crust is made up of 12 major plates. Heat from Earth's core influences the movement of these plates. The core heats the magma in the **mantle**, causing it to move. This movement forces the plates on the surface to shift. The shifting can cause mountains to rise where they did not previously exist. When this happens, mountains form in one of three ways.

Fold Mountains Scientists estimate that Earth's plates move only 4 inches (10 centimeters) a year. Although the plates move slowly, they constantly move toward or away from one another. When two plates push against each other, layers of rock in the plates are lifted and squeezed into arches or folds. The tops of the folds become the mountains that appear on Earth's surface. The Rockies and the European Alps are both fold mountain chains.

Fault-Block Mountains Cracks in Earth's surface are called faults. Faults form when Earth's crust is squeezed or stretched until it cracks. Some rocks are forced up, while others are pushed down. This action forms a fault-block mountain. Examples of fault-block mountain ranges include the Sierra Nevadas and White Mountains, both in the United States.

Volcanic Mountains Volcanic mountains form because of the movement of magma within Earth's mantle. As magma is heated by Earth's core, it moves toward the surface. In areas with volcanoes, the magma is pushed up with great force, called an eruption. In other places, where there is nowhere for the magma to escape, it causes a dome in Earth's crust. Examples of volcanic mountain ranges are the Cascade and Aleutian ranges of the United States.

Glacier's Plants

More than 1,500 types of plants can be found growing in Glacier National Park. These range from ground-hugging mosses to tall cedar trees. The wide variety of plants can be attributed to the large number of **habitats** in the park. Glacier's mountains, forests, and lakes each provide the necessary growing conditions for specific plants.

Forests cover approximately 55 percent of Glacier. About 90 percent of these forests are coniferous. The western hemlock and western red cedar are two of the park's most common coniferous trees. One of Glacier's most prevalent deciduous trees is the aspen. It grows at the park's lower elevations.

Almost 1,000 **species** of wildflowers grow in Glacier. The lowland areas are home to flowers such as clematises and purple asters. Beargrass and glacier lilies grow on the mountainsides. As colorful as the park's wildflowers are, some are dangerous to humans. Wolfsbane and milkweed are just two of the park's flower species that are poisonous if consumed.

Daisies are a common sight in Glacier. They can be found at elevations ranging from valley floors to subalpine forests.

GLACIER'S LIFE ZONES

While plants grow throughout Glacier, different elevations are home to specific types of vegetation. The areas where these plants grow are called life zones. Typically, the plants found in a zone share common characteristics and needs. Glacier has five distinct life zones.

Grasslands Found in the park's valleys and lower slopes, Glacier's grasslands zone contains more than 100 species of grass.

Aspen Parkland The aspen parkland zone marks the transition from grasslands to coniferous forests. Besides aspens and other deciduous trees, it features wetlands and marshes.

Montane Forest Known primarily for its coniferous trees, including Douglas firs and limber pines, the montane forest zone is found mainly at low to mid elevations.

Subalpine As the elevation increases, the thick coniferous forest disappears and is replaced with the dwarf trees and grassy meadows of the subalpine zone.

Alpine Tundra The alpine tundra zone is located above the **treeline**. Only small plants are found here. Most grow in low-lying mats.

Glacier's Wildlife

Glacier's many life zones also provide habitats for a variety of animals. The park is home to 277 species of birds and at least 66 mammal species, along with numerous reptiles, amphibians, fish, and insects. The number of plants and animals combined make Glacier a hotspot for **biodiversity**.

Most visitors to Glacier hope to catch a glimpse of one of the park's large mammals. Both grizzly and black bears roam the park's meadows and forests in search of berries. Bighorn sheep and mountain goats can often be spotted grazing on mountainsides.

Birds of all sizes can be seen flying around Glacier. American dippers dive into the park's rivers in search of fish to eat. Bald eagles soar high in the sky, their keen eyes scouring the land for rabbits and squirrels.

Glacier's rivers are home to both native and **invasive** fish. The lake trout was introduced to Glacier's waters in the early 1900s. As its population grows, it is taking food sources away from native fish such as the bull trout.

Mountain lions are one of Glacier's more secretive residents. They mainly hunt at night and are skilled at hiding among rocks and trees.

THE RETURN OF THE GRAY WOLF

Gray wolves were once found throughout Montana. However, in the 1800s, settlers from Europe and the eastern United States came to the area. They built towns and farms on the land. In doing so, they took over the wolves' habitat. This drove some wolves out of the area. Others were killed by the settlers, who saw them as pests. By the 1930s, Montana's wolf population had all but disappeared.

The loss of the gray wolves began to affect the **ecosystems** in places where they had lived. As **apex predators**, the wolves kept the populations of other animals, such as elk, under control. Efforts were made to bring gray wolves back to Montana.

While some areas had wolves shipped in from Canada, Glacier did not. After 50 years without wolves, a pack, believed to have come from Canada, set up a den in Glacier on their own in the 1980s. Since then, more packs have made Glacier their home.

Gray wolves may travel hundreds of miles (km) when trying to establish their own territory.

Founding Glacier

The founding of Glacier National Park is rooted in the arrival of European settlers in the area in the mid-1800s. Many of these early settlers came in search of furs, minerals, and other resources. Trading posts were set up, and communities grew around them.

In 1891, an extension of the Great Northern Railway was constructed through the mountains, making it easier for people from the East to visit. The tourism industry developed as more people came to Montana to take in its scenery. At first, tourists stayed in cabins built by the locals. Over time, hotels were built to accommodate the growing tourist trade.

Lake McDonald Lodge was one of the hotels built to accommodate the influx of tourists to Glacier. Constructed between 1913 and 1914, it was listed as a National Historic Landmark in 1987.

A man named George Bird Grinnell made his first visit to the area in 1885. The editor of a magazine called *Forest and Stream*, Grinnell wrote numerous articles describing the beauty of the region. He began to campaign for it to be made a national park. Others soon joined his efforts. In 1910, their wishes were granted when President William Howard Taft signed the bill that established the area as Glacier National Park.

BIOGRAPHY

George Bird Grinnell (1849–1938)

George Bird Grinnell was born into a wealthy New York family. As a boy, he was taught by Lucy Audubon, the wife of world-renowned **naturalist** John James Audubon. It is believed that Grinnell's love of nature came from the many hours he spent roaming the grounds of the Audubon estate in New York.

After graduating from Yale University in 1870, Grinnell took part in a fossil-finding expedition in the American West. His fascination with this part of the country led him to return to the area more than 40 times. Upon receiving his PhD in 1880, Grinnell embarked on a career as a naturalist. His role as editor of *Forest and Stream* gave him a platform to express his views on **conservation**.

Besides helping to create Glacier, Grinnell was instrumental in the development of the National Audubon Society, an organization devoted to the protection of birds and their habitats. He served as president of the National Parks Association as well. In 1925, Grinnell was awarded the Theodore Roosevelt Distinguished Service Medal for his conservation efforts.

FACTS OF LIFE

Born: September 20, 1849

Hometown: Brooklyn, New York

Occupation: Naturalist, writer, editor

Died: April 11, 1938

THE BIG PICTURE

In 1976, Glacier National Park was named a **biosphere** reserve by the United Nations Educational, Scientific, and Cultural Organization (UNESCO). Biosphere reserves are established to preserve an area's biodiversity while still allowing for the **sustainable** use of its resources. In total, there are currently 714 biosphere reserves around the world.

Glacier
United States

North America

Atlantic Ocean

Pacific Ocean

South America

Galapagos
Ecuador

Southern Ocean

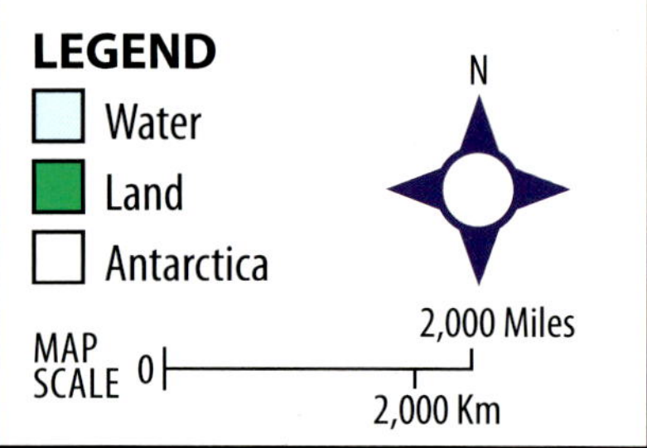

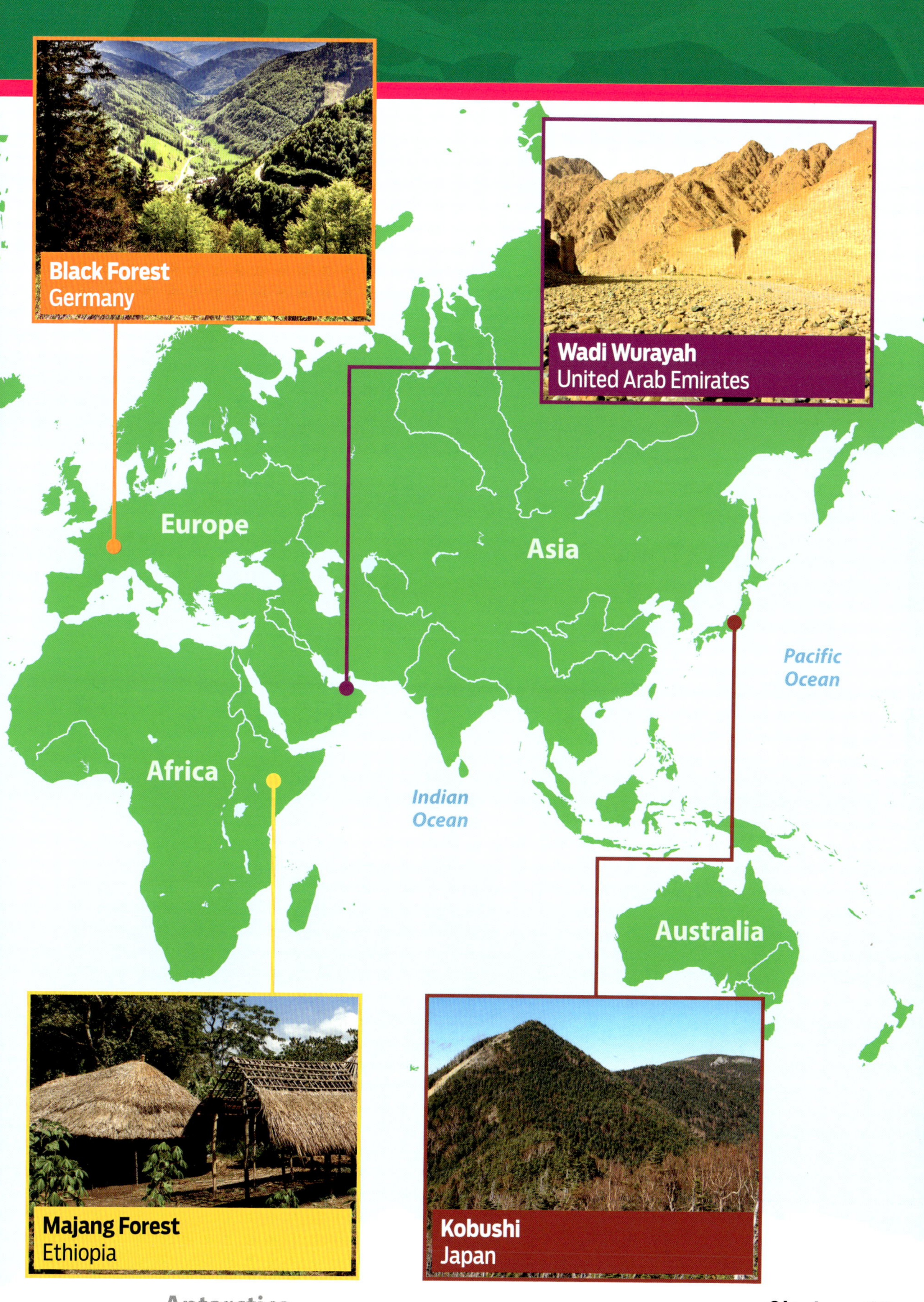
Black Forest
Germany
Wadi Wurayah
United Arab Emirates
Europe
Asia
Africa
Pacific
Ocean
Indian
Ocean
Australia
Majang Forest
Ethiopia
Kobushi
Japan
Antarctica

Peoples of Glacier

Aboriginal Peoples have lived in the area that is now Glacier National Park for at least 10,000 years. Ancestors of today's Blackfoot, Kootenai, Salish, and Pend d'Oreille hunted, fished, and held ceremonies on the land. When Europeans first arrived, the Blackfoot controlled the land east of the mountains. The Salish and Kootenai lived in the valleys and forests of the west.

These groups were only in the mountains at certain times of the year. The Blackfoot, for instance, would camp in low-lying areas for the winter. When spring came, the men would head to the prairies to hunt bison. The women and children would go to the mountains to collect roots and berries. When fall approached, they would return to their winter camps.

When Europeans arrived, they took land away from the Aboriginal Peoples for their settlements. The resources the Aboriginal Peoples relied on, especially the bison, became less plentiful. The Aboriginal Peoples turned to the U.S. government for help. They signed **treaties** that set aside land for them to live on. Called reservations, these lands are where many of the Blackfoot, Kootenai, Salish, and Pend d'Oreille live today.

The Blackfoot typically lived in teepees throughout the year. These homes were easy to erect and dismantle, making them ideal for families on the move.

PUZZLER

The Blackfoot depended on bison for their survival. Bison could be prepared as a food in different ways, including boiling, roasting, and drying. Dried bison meat was mixed with dried berries, pounded into a powder, and then mixed with fat to create pemmican. Stored in parfleches, or rawhide containers, pemmican would not spoil. This food helped the Blackfoot survive the area's long, cold winter.

Q. What were some of the other ways the Blackfoot used the bison they hunted?

ANSWER: The Blackfoot used materials from bison to make clothing, homes, tools, utensils, and weapons.

TIMELINE

80 million years ago

2.6 million years ago

10,000 years ago

1800

80 to 55 million years ago
The Rocky Mountains begin to form.

2.6 million to 11,700 years ago
Glaciers shape the Rockies during the ice age.

10,000 years ago
Ancestors of the Blackfoot, Kootenai, Salish, and Pend d'Oreille are living in the area.

Early 1800s
European trappers come to the region in search of beavers for the fur trade.

1885
George Bird Grinnell visits the area for the first time.

1891
A railroad over the Marias Pass is completed, making travel to the region easier. A tourist trade soon develops.

1976
Glacier is named a biosphere reserve by UNESCO.

1910 | 1950 | 1990 | 2020

1932
Glacier and Waterton form the world's first International Peace Park.

1910
President Taft signs a bill creating Glacier National Park.

2020
Glacier National Park celebrates its 110th birthday.

KEY ISSUE

SOUNDSCAPE NOISE

When most people come to a national park, they do so to get away from the stress of their daily lives. The park offers them a chance to relax and enjoy the peaceful sounds of a natural setting. Glacier, in particular, has a robust natural **soundscape** that includes roaring waterfalls, melodic birds, and chirping crickets. However, recent years have seen this soundscape change. The sounds of revving motorbikes and sightseeing helicopters flying overhead are interfering with the natural sounds of the park.

These actions can be disruptive to visitors to the park. They can also impact the park's wildlife. Animals rely on natural sounds to find mates, protect their young, and establish their territory. When other sounds get in the way, animal behavior changes. Some animals may feel threatened by the noise and decide to leave the area entirely.

Helicopter tours can cover a large area in a short amount of time, allowing visitors to see parts of the park they may not be able to access in other ways.

Should sightseeing helicopters be banned from flying over Glacier National Park?

Yes	No
Wildlife is being negatively impacted by the noise the aircraft create. Birds are having problems locating mates. Larger animals are moving out of certain areas.	People have the right to enjoy Glacier any way they choose. Flying over the park gives them a unique view into the park and its wildlife.
The helicopters are disrupting visitors who have paid to enter the park. As the aircraft are run by companies located outside the park, they should be required to stay outside the park.	The tours bring income to the park's outlying communities. In doing so, they help the local economy.

Glacier's staff are taking steps to educate visitors on the noise they make and how it affects others. For instance, brochures are being given to motorcyclists with tips on how to ride their bikes in the park. Park staff are having a more difficult time controlling the aircraft noise, however. This is because most of the sightseeing tours originate outside the park and are out of the jurisdiction of the National Park Service (NPS). The airspace over the park is controlled by the Federal Aviation Administration (FAA).

The park would like to see sightseeing aircraft prohibited from flying over Glacier. The NPS has been working with the FAA to put a plan together. Progress has been slow, and aircraft continue to fly over the park.

Park Attractions

Glacier offers visitors a variety of ways to experience the park. Outdoor enthusiasts can choose from an endless number of adventures. Sightseers can plan their own routes or take guided tours. History buffs can visit sites that showcase the park's past and its development over time.

Some of the park's earliest structures are its lodges. Built to accommodate tourists in the early 1900s, the lodges range from grand hotels to rustic cabins. One of the best-known of the grand lodges is Many Glacier Hotel. Named a National Historic Landmark in 1976, it sits along the shores of Swiftcurrent Lake at the base of Mount Grinnell.

Many of the buses used on the Red Bus Tours have been in service since the 1930s.

Many of the park's lodges serve as starting points for guided park tours. The park's Red Bus Tours were introduced in 1914. These buses visit all of the park's main attractions. This includes the scenic Going-to-the-Sun Road, which climbs the 6,646-foot (2,026-m) high Logan Pass.

For those who want to get off the beaten track, the park has many natural areas to explore. Hiking trails range from the family-friendly Fishercap Lake walking path to the more challenging Highline Trail. Glacier's many lakes are popular for boating and kayaking.

HIKING GLACIER

With 734 miles (1,181 km) of trails, it is no wonder that more than half of all visitors to Glacier go on a hike. Hiking is only enjoyable, however, when people come prepared for the activity. This means wearing the right clothes and bringing the right gear.

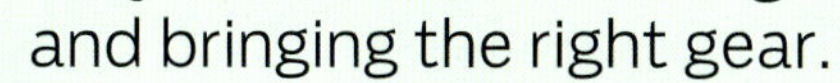

Wear sturdy footwear that will hold up on rough terrain.

Carry enough water to keep yourself hydrated for the full length of your hike.

Bear spray should be packed in case you encounter a bear on the trail.

Apply insect repellent before hiking and reapply throughout the day.

Sunscreen and a hat will help protect you from the Sun's rays.

Pack a meal, as well as snacks to eat along the way, to keep your energy level up.

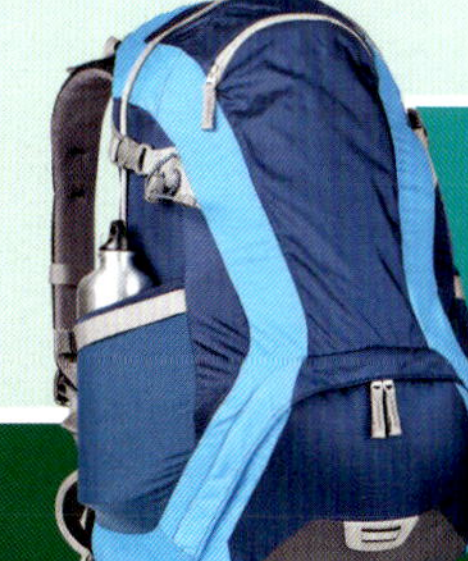

Bring a backpack to carry extra clothing, in case it rains or gets cold.

Cultural Heritage

Today, Aboriginal Peoples maintain a close connection to Glacier National Park. The Blackfeet Reservation is just east of the park. More than 8,000 Blackfoot live there.

Many Blackfoot welcome the opportunity to share their history and culture with visitors. The Blackfeet Trail Tour was put together to showcase the rich history of the Blackfoot. This self-guided tour takes people past areas where thousands of bison once roamed and traditional Blackfoot ceremonies were held.

The reservation is also home to the Museum of the Plains Indian. Founded in 1941, this museum features regalia and artifacts from many of the Native American groups that live on the Northern Plains. Creative works from both past and present artists are also on display.

The Blackfoot are one of the largest Native American nations in the United States. Their reservation covers an area of 1.5 million acres (607,000 ha).

THE LEGEND OF CHIEF MOUNTAIN

Chief Mountain towers over the prairies on the border between Glacier and the Blackfeet Reservation. This mountain stands separate from the other mountains. The Blackfoot have a strong, but tragic, connection to Chief Mountain.

Long ago, a Blackfoot warrior was named the war chief of his people. It was his job to lead them into battle. Shortly after he became war chief, he fell in love and married a local woman. They had a baby soon after. The warrior was so happy that he vowed never to go to war again.

One day, a Blackfoot war party went out to fight an enemy. Only four men returned. The war chief knew his people were in danger. He decided that he had to fight this enemy himself. Many warriors offered to fight with him. His wife asked to come as well. The war chief did not want to lose her. He convinced her to stay at the camp, in the shadow of the mountain.

The battle was fierce, but the Blackfoot were victorious. The war chief, however, was killed during the fighting. Overcome with grief, his wife took their child and climbed to the top of Chief Mountain. She threw herself and the child over the edge. The outline of a woman and child can be seen in the face of the mountain to this day.

Chief Mountain stands at the edge of the Rockies, where the prairies begin. This prominent location allows it to be seen from more than 100 miles (161 km) away.

WHAT HAVE YOU LEARNED?

TRUE OR FALSE?

Decide whether the following statements are true or false. If the statement is false, make it true.

1
Glacier National Park is home to more than 80 glaciers.

2
The Rockies are an example of fold mountains.

3
Glacier National Park was established during the presidency of President Calvin Coolidge.

4
UNESCO named Glacier a biosphere reserve in 1967.

5
The FAA controls the airspace over Glacier National Park.

6
Going-to-the-Sun Road climbs up Mount Grinnell.

ANSWERS

1. False. Glacier has only 26 glaciers.
2. True.
3. False. It was during William Howard Taft's presidency.
4. False. It became a biosphere reserve in 1976.
5. True.
6. False. It climbs Logan Pass.

SHORT ANSWER

Answer the following questions using information from the book.

1 How many people have visited Glacier since it opened?

2 When did the Rockies begin to form?

3 How much of Glacier is covered in forests?

4 When did wolves return to Glacier?

5 Who was the first person to campaign for Glacier to be a national park?

ANSWERS
1. More than 100 million
2. Between 80 and 55 million years ago
3. About 55 percent
4. In the 1980s
5. George Bird Grinnell

MULTIPLE CHOICE

Choose the best answer for the following questions.

1 What is the name of the park's largest glacier?

a. Harrison
b. Blackfoot
c. Jackson

2 When was the Waterton-Glacier International Peace Park founded?

a. 1935
b. 1929
c. 1932

3 Which of Glacier's life zones is located above the treeline?

a. Montane forest
b. Alpine tundra
c. Subalpine

4 What animal did the Blackfoot once depend on for their survival?

a. Gray wolf
b. Grizzly bear
c. Bison

ANSWERS
1. a 2. c 3. b 4. c

ACTIVITY

MAKE A MOUNTAIN

Rocks are formed and recycled through the movement of Earth's tectonic plates. Try this exercise below to see what happens to rocks when mountains form.

Materials

Instructions

1. Cut the foam into strips 2 to 4 inches (5 to 10 centimeters) wide and 8 to 12 inches (20 to 30 cm) long.
2. Using the scissors, cut two small holes into each end of the strips.
3. Alternate thickness and color to create a stack of three to five pieces. These layers of foam represent layers of rock.
4. Thread the string through the holes cut in the foam to fasten the pieces together, forming a foam sandwich.
5. Make sure the string is loose enough that the foam pieces can slide when bent. By pushing and folding the foam, you can imagine how rock layers respond to the same forces.

KEY WORDS

apex predators: animals that hunt others but are not hunted themselves

biodiversity: having a variety of life in a specific place

biosphere: the parts of Earth's crust, waters, and atmosphere that support life

climate change: a change in weather over a long period of time

conservation: the act of protecting something

ecosystems: communities of plants and animals living in the same place

glaciers: slow-moving sheets of ice

habitats: places where plants and animals live and grow

ice age: a period when sheets of ice covered large areas of the planet

invasive: something that intrudes or spreads itself in a harmful manner

mantle: the part of Earth found between the crust and the core

naturalist: a person who studies plants, animals, and other living things

soundscape: the sounds heard in a specific location

species: groups of living things that have common traits

sustainable: able to continue over a long period of time

tectonic plates: large pieces of Earth's crust

treaties: formal, binding agreements

treeline: the point on a mountain above which trees stop growing

watersheds: areas of land where all the surface water drains into the same place

INDEX

Get the best of both worlds.

AV2 bridges the gap between print and digital.

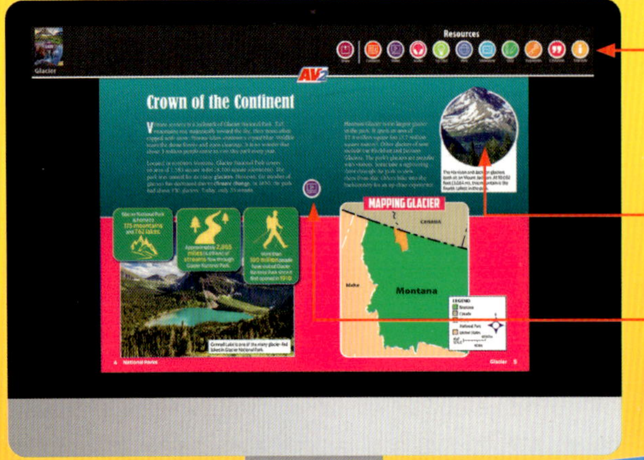

The expandable resources toolbar enables quick access to content including **videos**, **audio**, **activities**, **weblinks**, **slideshows**, **quizzes**, and **key words**.

Animated videos make static images come alive.

Resource icons on each page help readers to further **explore key concepts**.

Published by AV2
276 5th Avenue
Suite 704 #917
New York, NY 10001
Website: www.av2books.com

Library of Congress Cataloging-in-Publication Data

Names: Kissock, Heather, author.
Title: Glacier / Heather Kissock.
Description: New York, NY : AV2, [2022] | Series: National parks | Includes index. | Audience: Ages 10-13 | Audience: Grades 4-6
Identifiers: LCCN 2021012871 (print) | LCCN 2021012872 (ebook) | ISBN 9781791138516 (library binding) | ISBN 9781791138523 (paperback) | ISBN 9781791138530
Subjects: LCSH: Glacier National Park (Mont.)--Juvenile literature.
Classification: LCC F737.G5 K57 2022 (print) | LCC F737.G5 (ebook) | DDC 978.6/52--dc23
LC record available at https://lccn.loc.gov/2021012871
LC ebook record available at https://lccn.loc.gov/2021012872

Printed in Guangzhou, China
1 2 3 4 5 6 7 8 9 0 25 24 23 22 21

042021
101320

Project Coordinator Heather Kissock
Designers Tammy West, Ana Maria Vidal, and Terry Paulhus

Photo Credits
Every reasonable effort has been made to trace ownership and to obtain permission to reprint copyright material. The publisher would be pleased to have any errors or omissions brought to its attention so that they may be corrected in subsequent printings. AV2 acknowledges Getty Images, Alamy, Shutterstock, and Dreamstime as its primary photo suppliers for this title.